THE BIG BOOK OF CARTOONING

Drawing silly cartoon characters is a lot of fun! There is no right or wrong way to draw them. It's all up to you and your imagination!

Walter Foster Jr.

Quarto is the authority on a wide range of topics.
Quarto educates, entertains, and enriches the lives of our readers—
enthusiasts and lovers of hands-on living.
www.quartoknows.com

© 2016 Quarto Publishing Group USA Inc.
Published by Walter Foster Jr., an imprint of Quarto Publishing Group USA Inc.
All rights reserved. Walter Foster Jr. is trademarked.
Artwork © Dave Garbot
Illustrated and written by Dave Garbot

6 Orchard Road, Suite 100
Lake Forest, CA 92630
quartoknows.com
Visit our blogs at quartoknows.com

This book has been produced to aid the aspiring artist. Reproduction of work for study or finished art is permissible. Any art produced or photomechanically reproduced from this publication for commercial purposes is forbidden without written consent from the publisher, Walter Foster Jr.

MIX
Paper from
responsible sources
FSC® C101537

Printed in China
1 3 5 7 9 10 8 6 4 2

Table of Contents

Getting Started

We're almost ready to get this show on the road.
Even if this is your first time drawing, this book
will be a lot of fun and something you can use over
and over again. So smile big, grab your pencil and
paper, and let's start cartooning!

What You Will Need

crayons

eraser

colored pencils

markers

pencil

Drawing paper

Cartoon characters use lots of accessories. Here are a few ideas to keep in mind as you draw.

ead Shapes

Here are some basic head shapes.
We'll use some of these examples later.

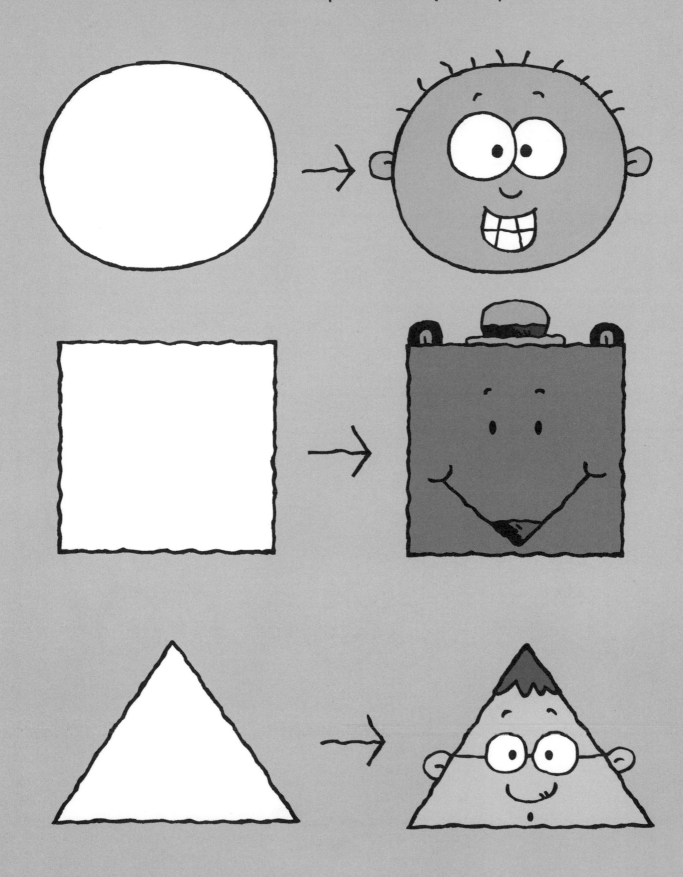

Funny Faces

Here are a few facial features you can use on your cartoon characters. What do you want them to look like? Crazy? Zany? Scary? Surprised? You decide!

Eyes

Eyes can be goofy, sleepy, and mysterious (yikes!). They can be different sizes or even just simple dots.

Noses

Noses, beaks, snouts, and schnozzes can be different shapes too.

Mouths

Mouths can be a simple squiggle; an unhappy frown; or a great, big, cheesy grin!

Expressions

Expressions can tell a lot about our characters and how they feel. They are usually pretty happy, but maybe the character you draw is tired, surprised, or extra excited! You can use facial expressions and gestures to help express emotions and personality.

Happy

Sick

Confused

Worried

Amused

Surprised

Excited

Tired

Angry

Embarrassed

Content

Sad

Curious

The Color Wheel

The color wheel shows us how colors relate to one another. Artists use the color wheel to understand the different colors and how to mix them.

There are three primary colors: red, yellow, and blue. These colors cannot be made by mixing other colors. But with these three colors, you can mix just about any other color you want!

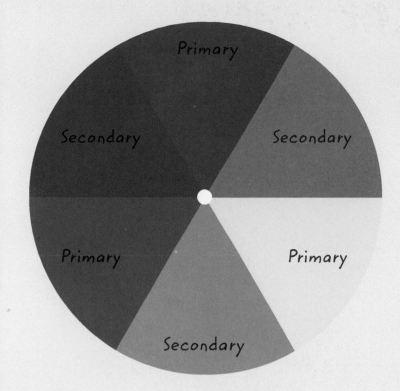

Primary

Secondary   Secondary

Primary   Primary

Secondary

By mixing two primary colors, you can create a secondary color! Orange, green, and purple are secondary colors.

 +  =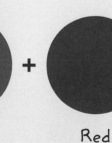

Red   Yellow   Orange

 + =

Blue   Red   Purple

 + =

Yellow   Blue   Green

Complementary Colors

Complementary colors sit on opposite sides of the color wheel. Complementary colors make each other look good when they are used together!

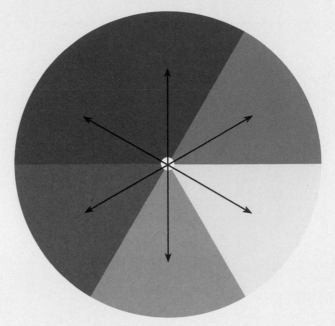

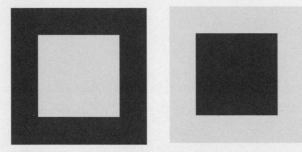

Look how vibrant the complementary yellow and purple squares are.

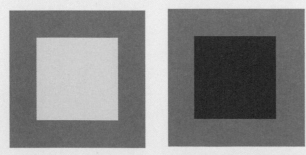

These squares are not as vibrant. That's because yellow and purple are complementary colors!

Complementary (kom-pluh-men-tuh-ree) colors make each other look brighter!

See just how much Beastly Beauty Queen's yellow sash pops against her purple dress?

Orange and blue are complementary colors. Surfing Sunny's bright shorts help him stand out while he's riding those epic waves.

Red and green are complementary colors, which is probably why Digger looks so snazzy in his suit.

Spectacular Superheroes

Super! Mighty! Amazing! These are all words we use to describe superheroes. They use their special powers to come to the rescue and save the day! They can be very serious, but they like to smile too! In this section, we'll learn to draw super characters that are fun, wacky, and just plain silly. Grab your mask, your cape, and your pencil, and let's use our super drawing powers to have some fun!

SUPER FEATURES

Here are a few basic features you can use if you want your superhero to have a different look. You can practice drawing your own and come back to this page if you need ideas.

Practice drawing some super features.

Batty Man

Our hero has his bat-o-rang with him, but maybe he should be holding something else. How about a fish or a banana?

23

Kat Woman

Mice usually stay away from cats, but our hero has the cheese! Can you add two, three, or maybe ten more mice to this scene?

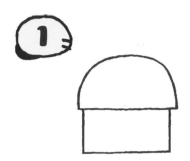

25

Super Hippo

Our hero looks pretty happy. Will he look more serious if you change his eyes? Go back to page 10 if you need ideas.

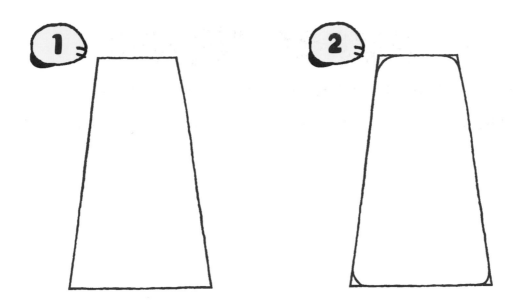

Wonder Gal

Wonder Gal and Spike are ready for action! Do you think Wonder Gal needs more stars on her outfit? How about Spike? How would they look with silly hats?

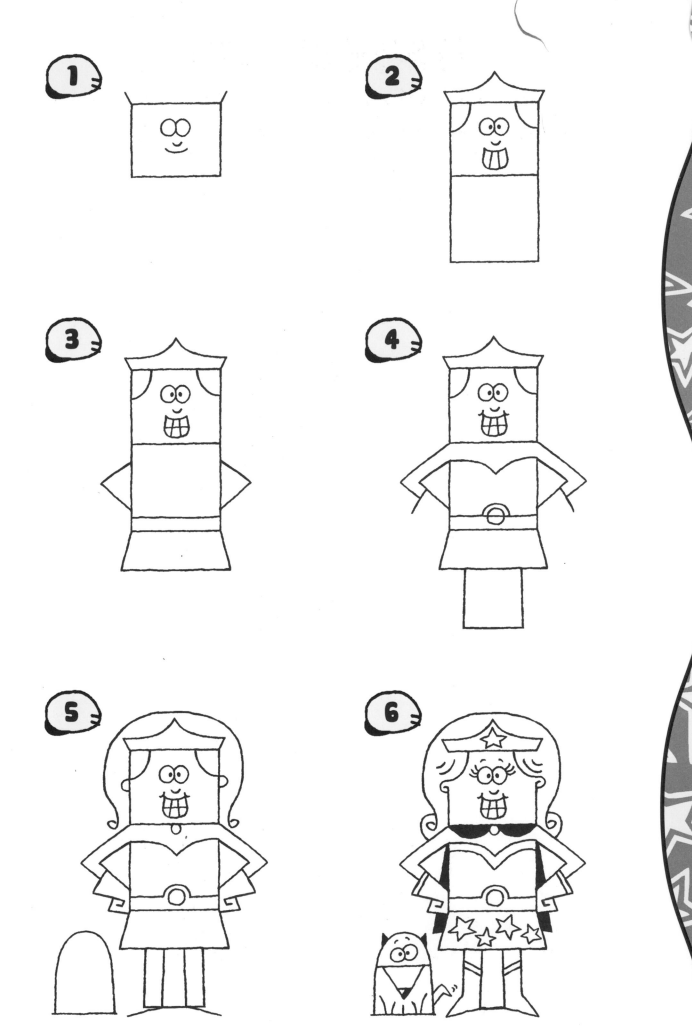

HULK

Yikes! Hulk looks pretty upset. How can you make him look a little happier? Hint: Draw a smile! Check out page 20 if you need ideas!

Aqua Dude

Now that you've practiced your super drawing skills, can you complete the drawings below? Get creative! Add a few fish to Aqua Dude's seaweed hair, or draw a taco in his hand. What else can you add?

The Flash

The flash is FAST! Start out with this simple shape, tilting everything forward to make him seem like he's moving fast! Can you give him roller blade boots to make him even faster?

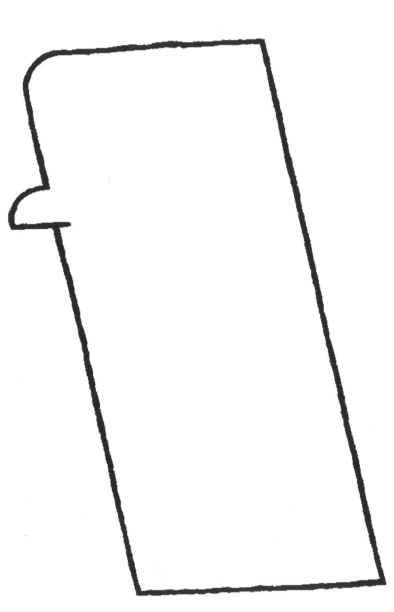

Awesome Aliens

Now we're ready to draw some out-of-this-world creatures! Some will have five eyes, and some will have only one. You never know with aliens because they're all so different, which makes them a lot of fun to draw! So grab your pencil and maybe a cookie or two (because aliens really love cookies), and let's see what kind of kooky extraterrestrials we can create!

Stellar Features

Here are a few things you can use when drawing your aliens. Maybe you'll want different eyes, a silly mouth, or crazy ears. You can practice drawing your own features and come back to these pages if you need Sparky's help to come up with a few new ones.

Practice drawing some stellar features.

Moobambo

How would he look with no arms and more eyes?
Try making the eyeballs different sizes!

Xebo 5 & Snert

This is a crazy pair! Can you give Xebo 5 a few more ears and another mouth? How about an extra tail for Snert?

41

Altacon

This Robo alien is blasting off! Try drawing the groundline even lower to make him look like he's high in the air!

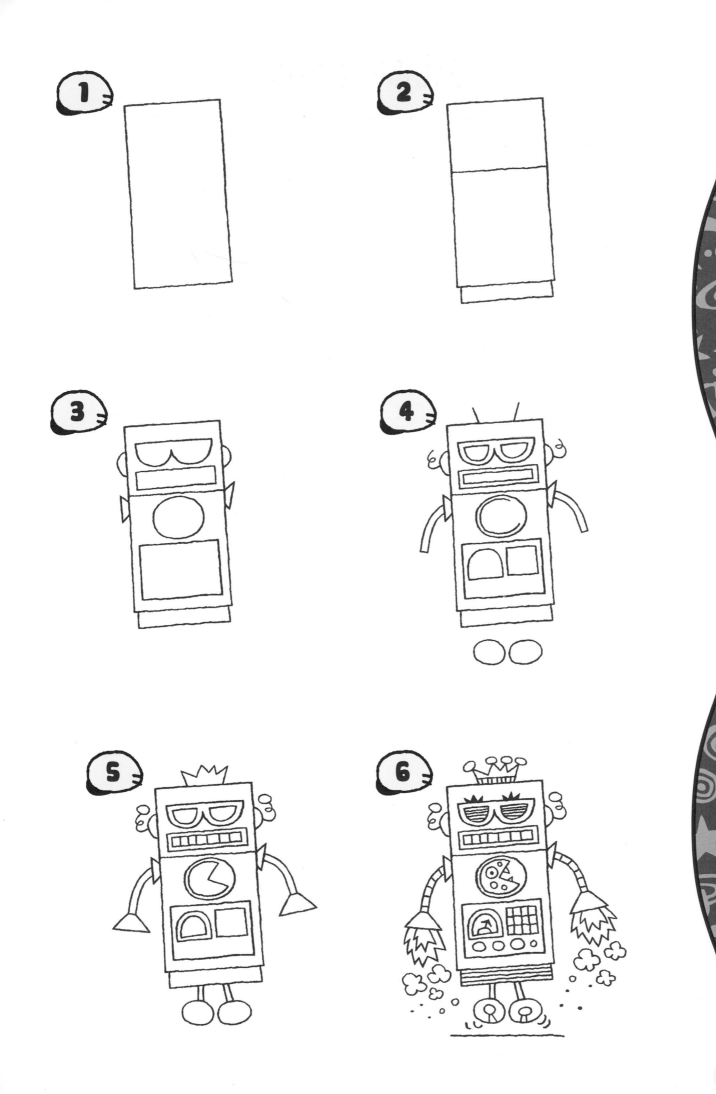

1

2

3

4

5

6

MoMa BLip

How would this alien look without her helmet? Can you make more mini aliens for MoMa Blip to keep track of?

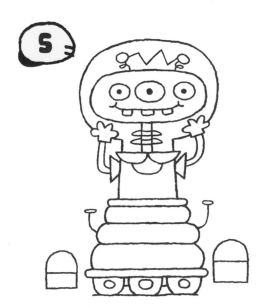

45

Slugbotu

Six eyes, but only two arms? How would he look with another pair of arms? How about another mouth or two? This alien is like a worm, so your lines can be extra wiggly if you want!

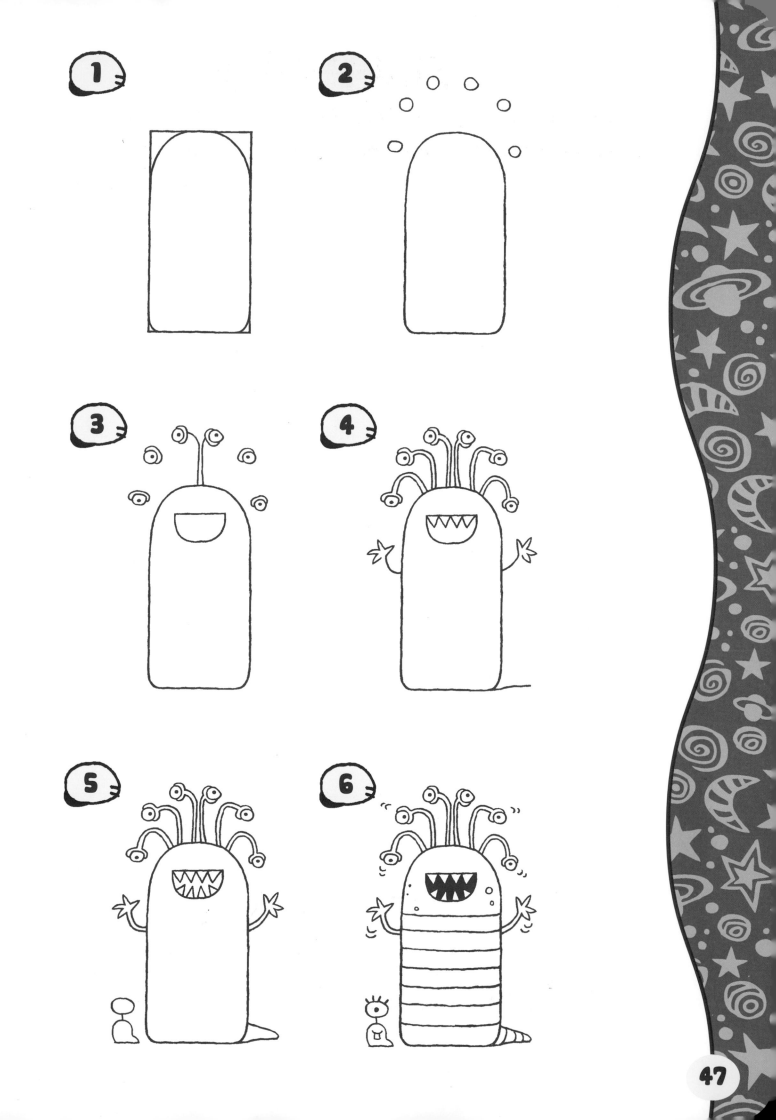

47

Fleeb

Now that your drawing skills are truly out-of-this-world, let's practice finishing the drawings below. Fleeb has five eyes! How would he look with one big eye instead? How about one tiny one? Don't worry too much about the shape of his head—it's OK that it looks like a big potato!

Glogdoss

Can you make this creature another color? How would he look with a smaller eye? What if his cell phone was a cookie?

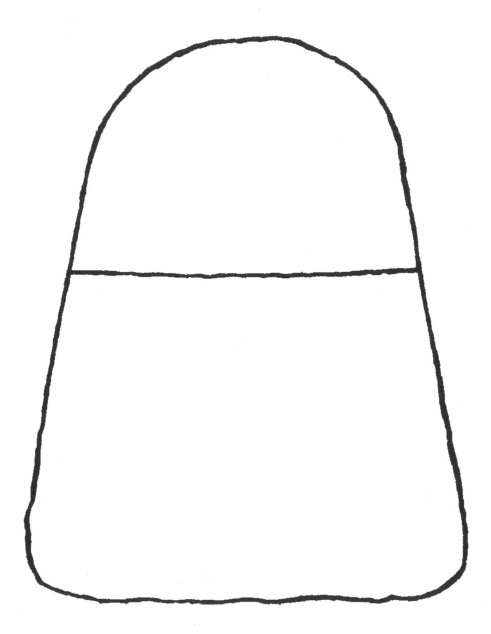

Furry & Feathered Friends

In this section, we'll draw some feathered friends and characters who are just too cute to handle—they're guaranteed to make you smile! As you draw these animals, remember that they come in all colors, shapes, and sizes. Think of how sweet they are, and maybe you can add an accessory or two to make them even more adorable! They won't mind at all!

Funny Features

Here are a few basic features you can use when drawing furry and feathered animals. Use this page to practice drawing your own features, and come back for more ideas if you want to give your character a different look.

Practice drawing some funny features.

Digger

Digger looks pretty spiffy in his jacket. Can you change the colors and patterns on his clothes? How would Digger look with different eyes?

Henrietta

Whoa...those are some crazy socks and shoes! Can you add a hat? Start your drawing with simple rectangles, and then use your eraser to give Henrietta her shape.

chirp!

chirp!

Milton Moose

Should Milton have more bird friends, or fewer? You decide! To draw his head, start with a pear-like shape that isn't quite oval.

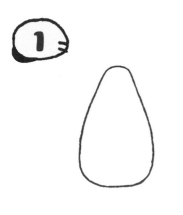

Square Head Bear

This bear wears a tie to work every day, but all you need to draw him are simple shapes. Follow the steps on the opposite page to draw Square Head Bear.

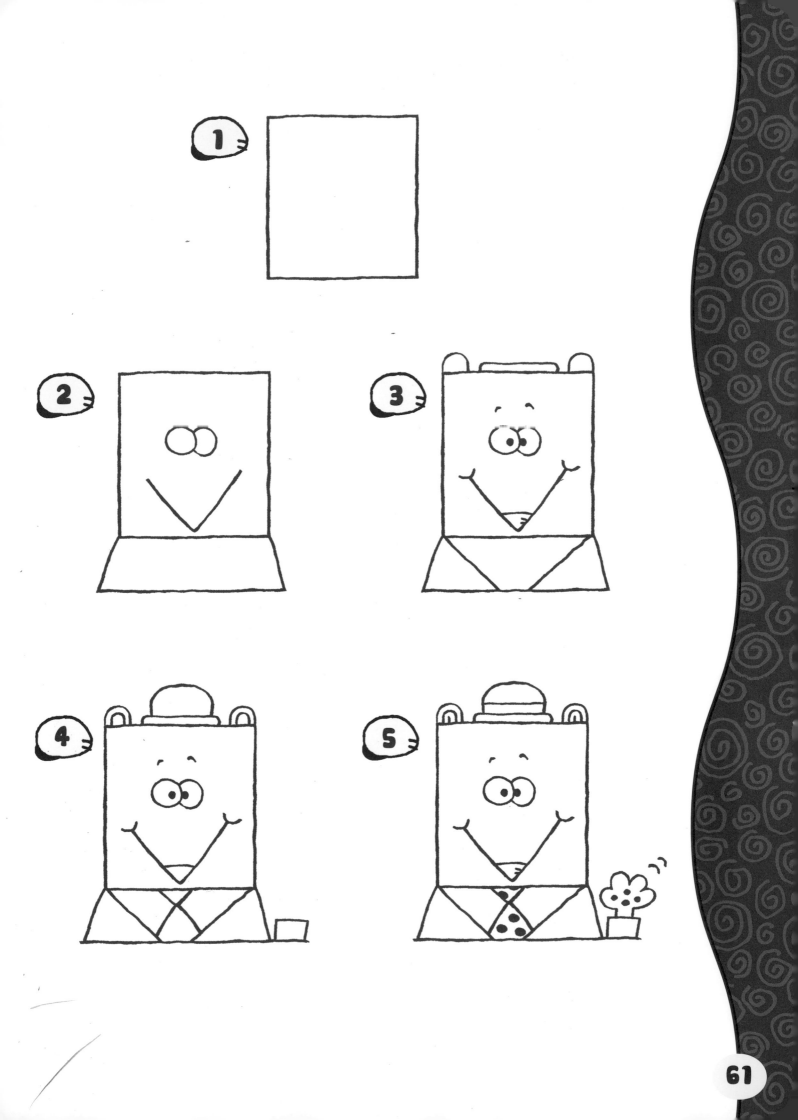

61

Percy Panda

Pandas are usually black and white, but if you use your imagination, this one can be blue, yellow, or even pink!

Kit Cat

Practice drawing more cute animals by completing the drawings below. This kitty has a football-shaped head. Can you give her a pretty bow to wear? A collar with bells? It looks like she could use some company. How about drawing a mouse friend for her to play with?

Perky Penguin

The thing about penguins is that you always seem to see more than just one! After you draw this penguin, can you use different accessories and color to create even more? Give his friends matching hats or musical instruments so they can start a band. Whatever you do, rock on!

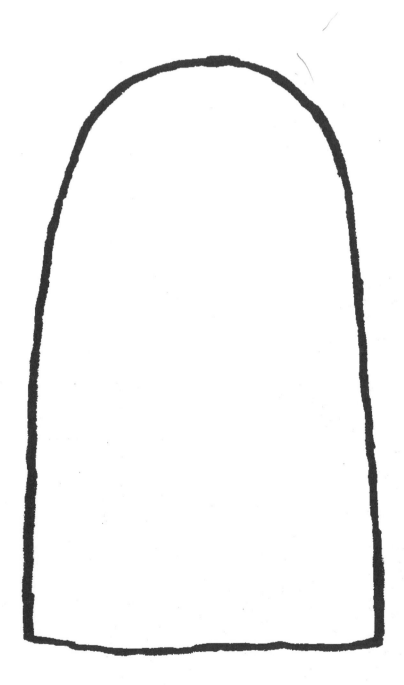

Silly Sports

Do you like to play soccer, skate, or run? Maybe you like to race cars or ride your bicycle. Many people enjoy sports and sometimes play more than one! Whatever you like to do, the most important thing is to have fun. In this section, we'll take some favorite sports and learn to draw the characters that play them, but with a little extra silliness too! On your mark, get set...draw!

Silly Features

Here are a few things you can use when drawing your characters. Maybe you'll want a curly hairdo, crazy eyeballs, or a bushy beard for your sports hero! It's all up to you. Come back to these pages any time you need some ideas and practice.

Practice drawing your own silly features.

soccer Susie

Can you give Susie a different kind of ball to kick?
If she kicks the ball forward instead of back over her head,
how would you draw her eyes?

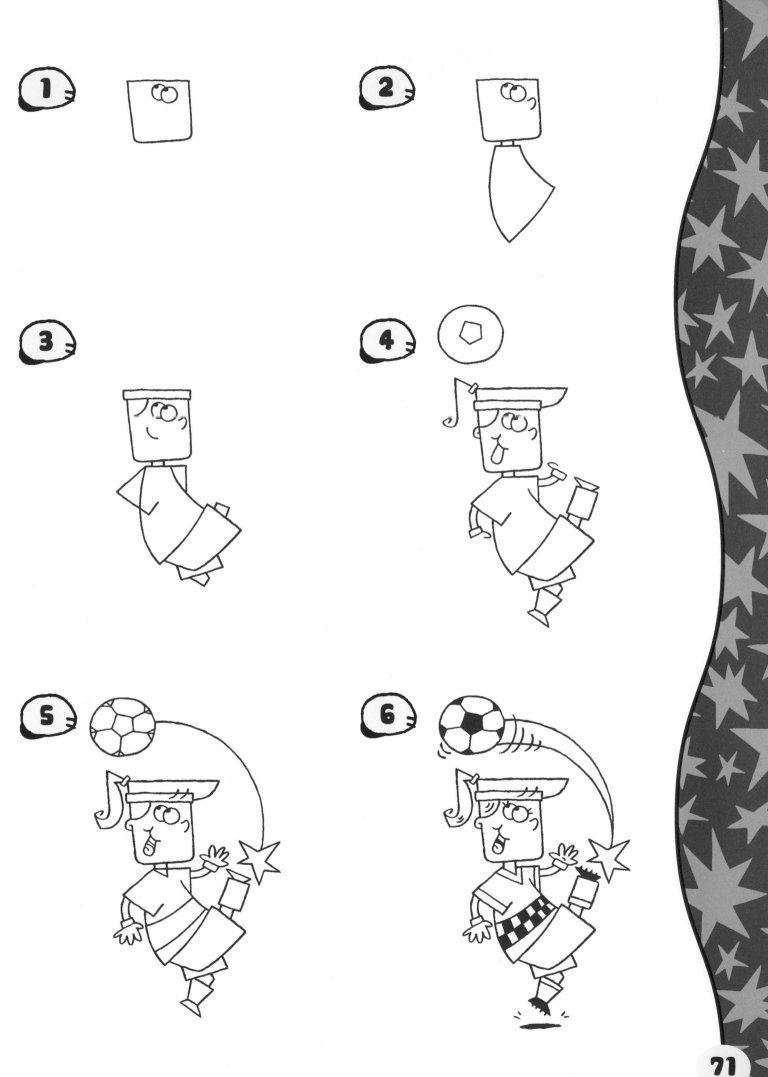

Running Randy

This track star might look pretty silly with fluffy slippers on his feet! Once you draw one runner, draw another one, two, or maybe even five more behind him to make it a big race!

Gymnast Gemma

Do you think Gemma could balance something on her head while she performs? How about a bird, a plant, or a bunny? When you're done, try drawing Gemma in a different pose.

Bicycling Betty

That is a crazy-looking helmet. How about adding some fancy ribbons to the bike handles to really make her fly!

Car Racing Robbie

Can you add a cool design to this racer's car and helmet? Adding the groundline below the wheels and little puffs of dust and rocks in the last step will make your racer look like he's really moving!

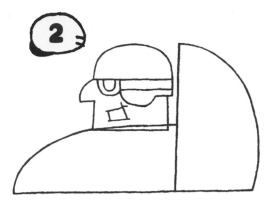

Ice skating Sally,

Now let's practice completing the characters below. Can you draw Sally with her eyes open? How about with a different hat and mittens? If you draw the groundline a little lower, it will look as if she's jumping in the air!

Roller Derby Debbie

This tough roller gal looks a little wobbly. Try drawing her with both skates on the ground.

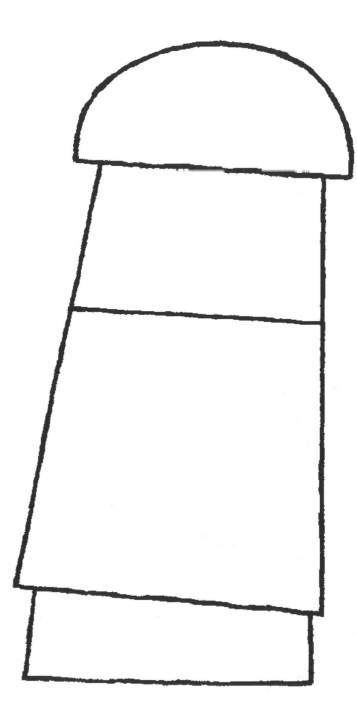

Mean 'N' Messy Monsters

Drawing can be kind of scary when you're first starting out. But when you're drawing monsters, you don't have to worry whether your lines are perfectly straight—the messier and squigglier the better! Follow the steps and your monster will appear right before your very eyes (or eye)!

The Monster Shop

Hello. I'm Ignatius, but you can call me Iggy. I work here in the Monster Shop, keeping an eye on all those features you may need when drawing your "friends." Look around, and use anything you like. If you don't like it, you can always bring it back, or better yet, just erase it!

Practice drawing a few monstrous features.

Spidey

Spidey has decided to wear a hat, but you can take it off if you like, or give him a different one. Do you have a favorite kind of hat that you would like him to wear?

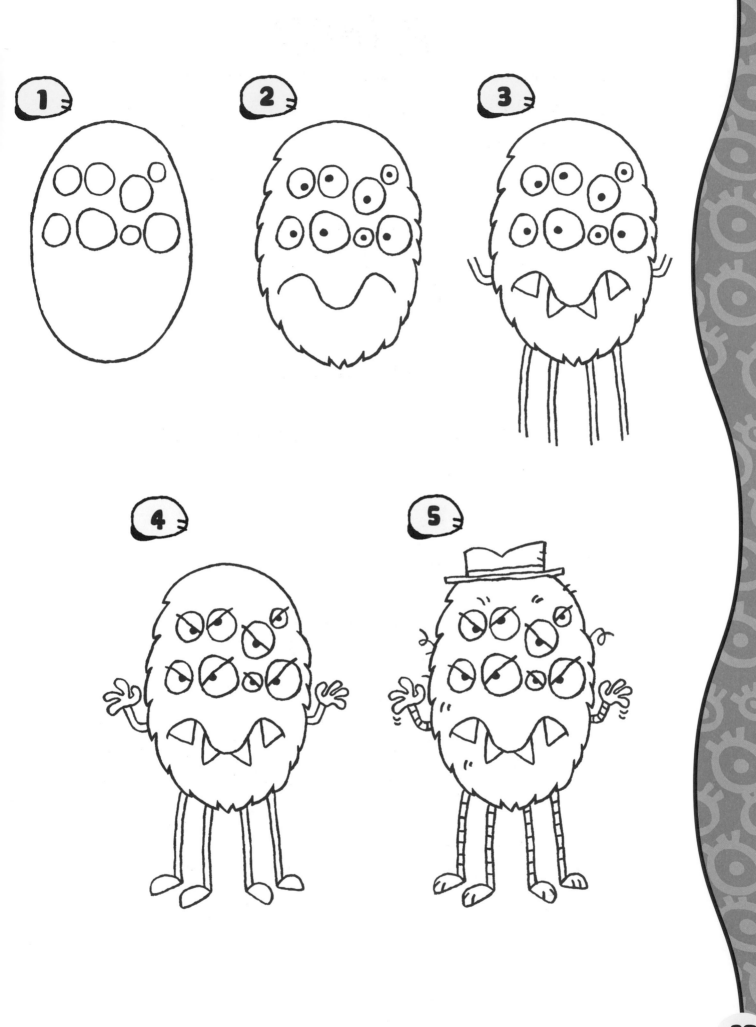

Frankie

Frankie is wearing his sneakers, but how would he look if you took his shoes off and added different feet? Go back to page 84 if you need ideas!

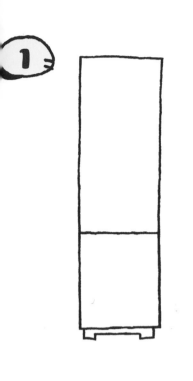

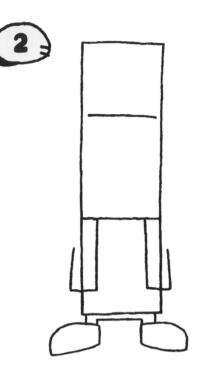

Mertle

Can you draw three more Mertles,
each one a little different from the others?

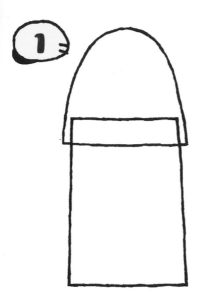

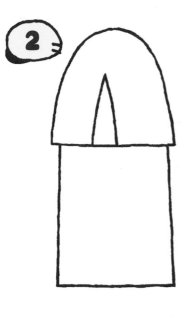

Draco

Draco looks pretty spiffy in this tuxedo. He must be going to a party! Add another character to your drawing so he won't have to go alone! How about a party hat too?

Godzilla

When you're done, try coloring Godzilla a different color.
Maybe give him some spots too!

stinky Foot

Pee-yew! This foot monster sure is stinky, and he's not too happy about it. How do you make people notice? Can you add a few flies buzzing through the air or overgrown nails to each of his toes? It's your drawing, so you decide!

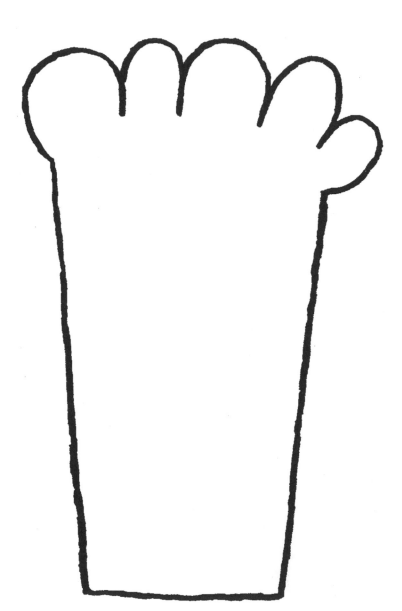

Fishy

Fishy likes to eat worms. Yuck! Can you add a few coming out of his mouth to make him happy? What else can you add? Scales and fins? Bubbles?

Fairy Tale Fun

Fairy tales are always fun to read and listen to. However, since fairy tales are just stories, we have to use our imaginations or rely on the illustrations of an artist to help us follow along. In this section, we'll do just that. We'll learn to draw many of the characters we've read about before, but with a silly twist to give them tons of personality. Let's get started!

Fantastic Features

Here are a few things you can use when drawing your characters.
Maybe you'll want a different hairstyle, a beard, or fancy shoes!
Come back to this section to practice and gather ideas.

Practice drawing your own fantastical features.

Red Riding Hood

What if Red had a different color cape and hood? Then what would her name be? Start your drawing off with a simple circle, but don't worry if it's not perfectly round.

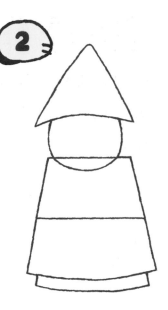

Prince Charming

Look! The prince has found a glass slipper. Can you change it to something else? How about a cheeseburger?

Drake Dragon

Some fairy tale dragons like to fly. Try adding wings so this one can take off!

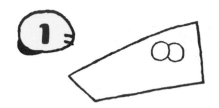

Pinky Unicorn

Can you draw this pretty unicorn with its eyes open?

Robin Hood

Robin looks pretty happy. Can you give him different eyes?
How about a different mouth?

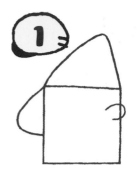

1

2

3

4

5

6

7

The Three Bears

The fairy tale characters on these pages usually come in threes. Can you finish each one? These bears are so cute. Looking back at some of the lessons we've already completed, do you think you could draw Goldilocks to join them? Maybe dress the bears in crazy costumes or give them new accessories!

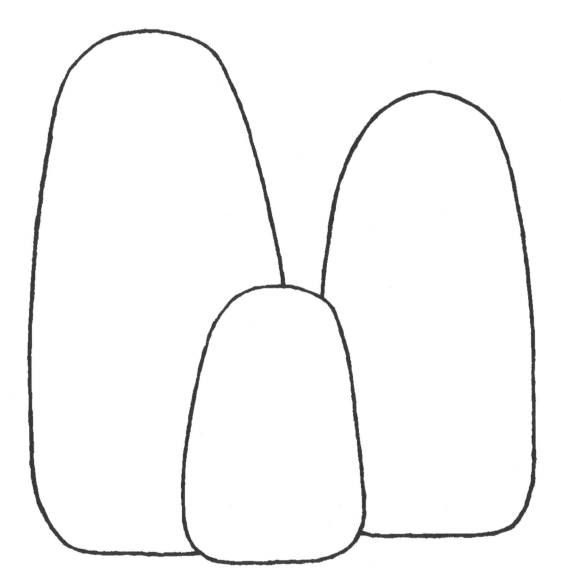

The Three Little Pigs

Here's one little pig, but can you draw his two friends?
Pig 1 can hold a piece of straw, Pig 2 can hold sticks,
and Pig 3 can hold...what?

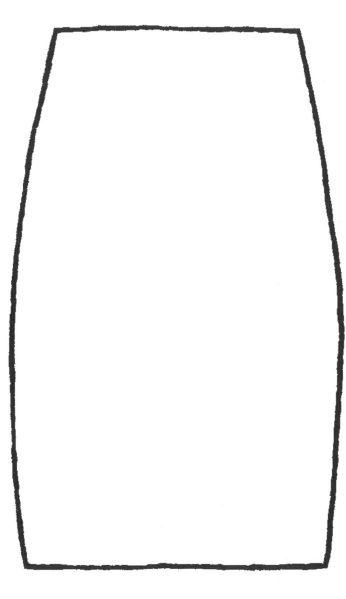

Now that you are a cartooning master, the sky is the limit! Use what you've learned to make your own characters. A hippo with wings? A monster mailman? Take something ordinary and make it EXTRAordinary. And just for fun, enjoy coloring the cartoon creations on the following pages. Go back to page 14 if you need to refresh your knowledge of the color wheel.

super Dino

VULBLUB

Hoots

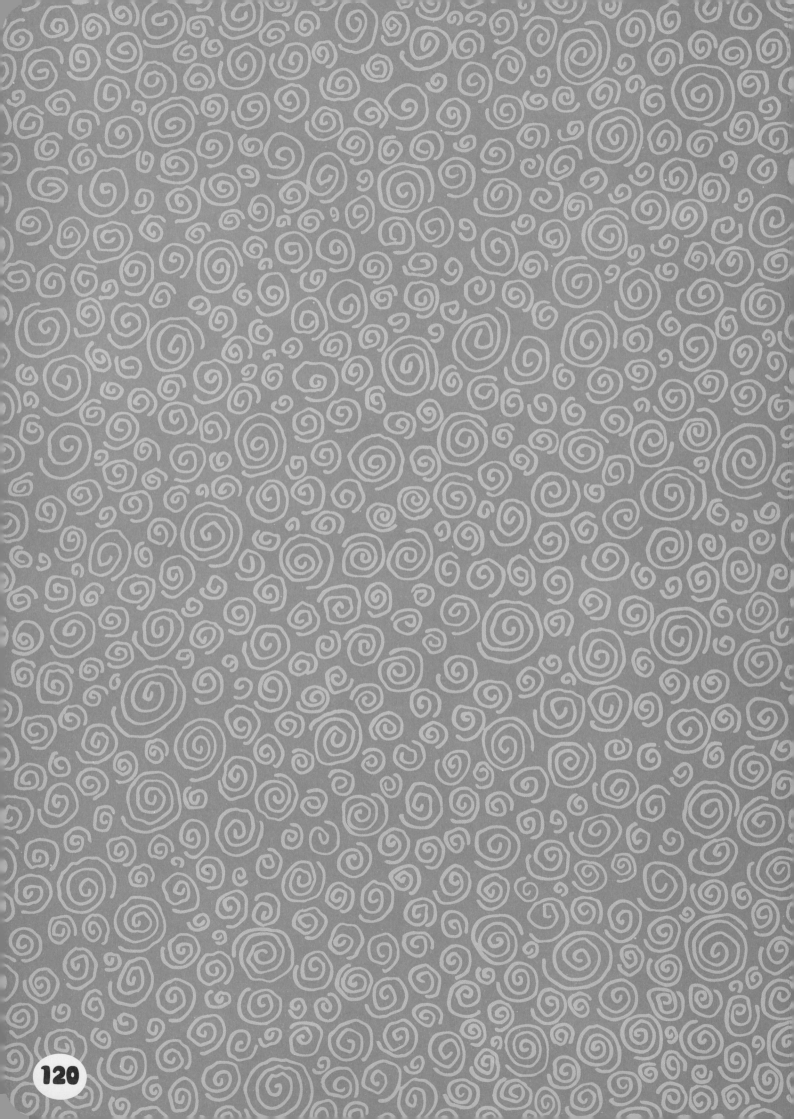

scuba diving steve

Wilma the Witch

Pretty Princess

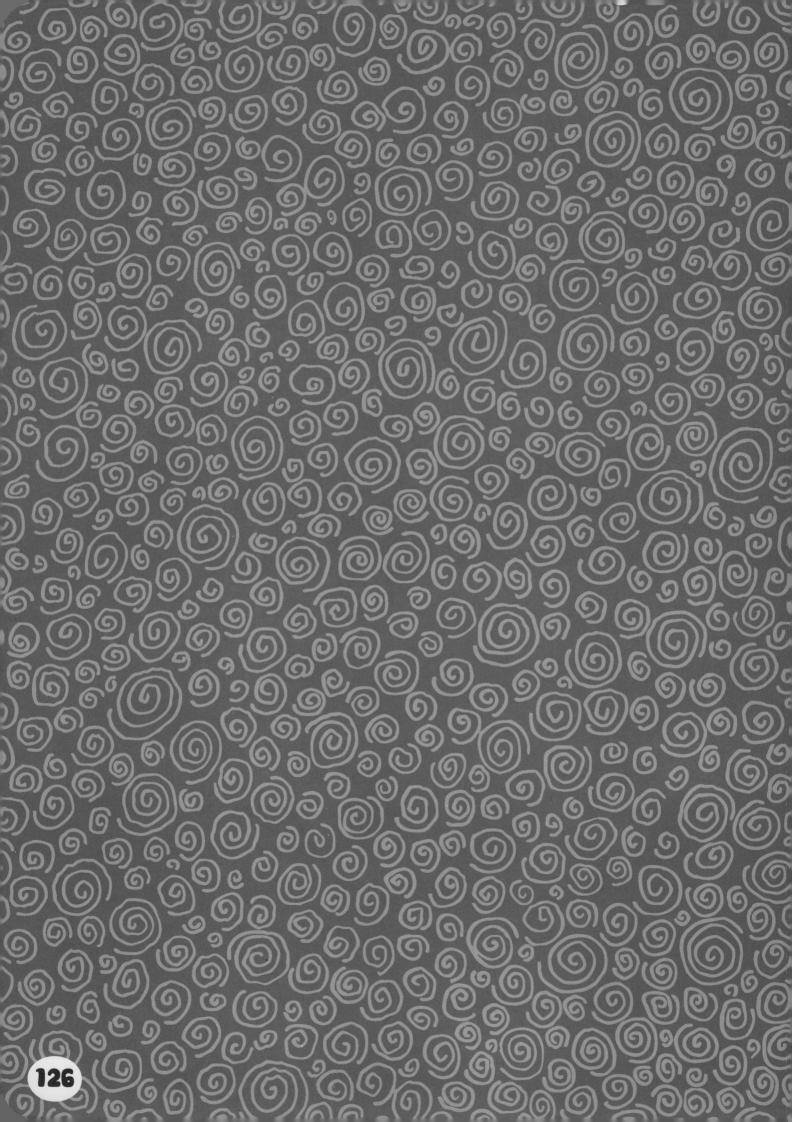

Betty Ballerina

About the Author

Dave Garbot is a professional illustrator and has been drawing for as long as he can remember. He is frequently called on to create his characters for children's books and other publications. Dave always has a sketchbook with him and gets many of his ideas from the things he observes every day, as well as from lots of colorful childhood memories. Although he admits that creating characters brings him personal enjoyment, making his audience smile, feel good, and maybe even giggle is what really makes his day.